The Candy Castle

Deep in the forest lived some happy, peaceful, and helpful fairies. Each day they would search and collect food for their meals, and stored the extras in a hollow tree.

One day, when the fairies flew deep into the forest to gather food, one of the youngest fairies flew off in another direction and got lost.

When it was time to return home, they noticed that she was not with the group. All the fairies searched and searched, but could not find her.

So, before evening fell, the fairies decided to build a pathway to their home. They knew the young fairy would see the shiny stones because they looked just like her favorite candies.

At night these special stones lit up, and would provide enough light so the fairy could find her way back home.

The young fairy flew and flew over the forest, but could not find her friends. It was getting dark now, and she was very tired.

She saw a large hollow tree where she could sleep for the night. The young fairy took the food that she had gathered and climbed into the tree to sleep.

Before sunrise, the other fairies began their search for the young fairy. Some flew high above the trees, some flew in the middle of the trees while others searched on foot on the ground.

Only an hour had gone by when one fairy spotted a foot hanging out a hollow tree. "Here she is," she shouted.

Since it was early in the morning, the little fairy was still asleep, but all the excitement woke her up. Now, with all the fairies accounted for, they headed home.

Later that day, the older fairies wondered how to keep younger fairies from getting lost in the forest. There were several great suggestions, but the best one was to build a Candy Castle out of the shiny stones that were used for the pathway.

The second best suggestion was to build the castle high enough so that fairies would be able to see it when flying high above the trees, and wide enough so that fairies would be able to see it when flying close to the ground.

Then they looked for a perfect place to build the castle. They found a spot of land with a small brook running with cool water, and berry bushes on both side of the brook.

All agreed that it was a special location, and started to build their Candy Castle. The fairies gathered stones of all different colors, sizes, and shapes.

The new castle was large enough to store all of the food that was gathered during the summer, berries, nuts and apples, and some wild greens.

The fairies lived deep in the forest, and never came into contact with human beings, but they were aware of them.

Each year before fall, people would come to have fun camping, hiking, and picnicking in the forest before the weather got cold, and days got shorter.

**_No one knew this year
would be different._**

Soon, some visitors stopped to camp in the forest. They thought that their two little boys would enjoy the adventure of hiking and cooking out in nature before returning home.

That night, the two brothers counted the stars in the sky before they went to sleep, and enjoyed the fresh clean air. They could not wait until morning to see what adventures they were going to have.

In the morning the family ate breakfast, and while their mother was cleaning up the boys packed a small lunch and went hiking with their father.

They climbed some mountains that looked over the entire forest. When they returned to camp, it was time for supper.

After eating, the two boys asked if they could play before going to bed. Their parents give them permission but reminded them not to go too far in the forest.

The brothers thanked their parents and took off running to play hide and seek.

Each time one brother would put his hands over his eyes, count to ten and took off to find the other. This went on for a while until they realized that each game had taken them farther and farther into the forest.

It was getting dark, and the boys knew they were lost. They called their parents but their mother and father did not answer.

At the same time, their parents were also calling out for them, "Joseph"! "Jacob"! But, there was no response from the brothers.

The two boys began to cry softly, as the walked deeper and deeper into the forest. While searching for a way back to their parents, one brother saw shiny stones on the ground. It reminded him of candy, and he thought this could be a pathway back to camp.

Both boys started to follow the stones and came upon the beautiful Candy Castle. They really got excited to see the fresh berries to eat and cool water to drink. They were hungry and thirsty, so they started to eat.

When the boys finished eating they looked up to see the fairies standing by, and they got scared. The fairies comforted the brothers by telling them that they would help them out of the forest, and back to their parents in the morning.

The fairies give them a place to sleep, and warm milk to drink for pleasant dreams. The boys slept peacefully. In the morning they were eager to see their parents.

As promised, the fairies guided the brothers back to their parents. Standing off in the distance, the fairies watched as the boys were greeted with lots of hugs and kisses.

Their father finished packing up the car while the brothers ate breakfast and told about their adventure.

The fairies stayed to watch as the car disappeared down the road.

All of the fairies realized that it was an excellent idea building the Candy Castle because it could help both young children and young fairies find their way home.

Special Thanks

Thanks to my family for encouraging me to express myself in writing and especially to my Auntie Barbara for editing my first children's book.

Dedication

This book is dedicated to all families that have experienced loss of their loved ones and are unable to establish closure.

The End